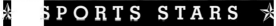

EMMITT SMITH

FINDING DAYLIGHT

By Ted Cox

CP CHILDRENS PRESS®
CHICAGO

Photo Credits

Cover, ©Stephen Dunn/Allsport USA; 6, ©Don Smith/Sports Photo Masters, Inc.; 9, ©Jeff Carlick/Sportschrome East/West; 10, Focus On Sports; 13, Reuters/ Bettmann; 14, Focus On Sports; 17, ©Rich Kane/Sportschrome East/West; 18, UPI/Bettmann; 20, 23, ©Tom DiPace/Focus On Sports; 24, 27, 28, Reuters/Bettmann; 31, ©Stephen Dunn/Allsport USA; 32, Focus On Sports; 33, ©Bob Ewell/Sports Photo Masters, Inc.; 35, ©Louis A. Raynor/ Sports Photo Masters, Inc.; 37, 39, Focus On Sports; 40, Reuters/Bettmann; 43, ©Bob Ewell/Sports Photo Masters, Inc.; 44, ©Mike Powell/Allsport USA; 47, Focus On Sports

Project Editor: Shari Joffe
Design: Beth Herman Design Associates
Photo Research: Jan Izzo

Library of Congress Cataloging-in-Publication Data

Cox, Ted.
    Emmitt Smith: finding daylight / by Ted Cox.
      p. cm. – (Sports stars)
    ISBN 0-516-04383-8
    1. Smith, Emmitt–Juvenile literature. 2. Football players–
United States–Biography–Juvenile literature. 3. Dallas Cowboys
(Football team)–Juvenile literature. [1. Smith, Emmitt. 2. Football
players.] I. Title. II. Series.
GV939.S635C68   1994
796.332'092–dc20
[B]   93-43837
                                          CIP
                                          AC

SPORTS STARS

EMMITT SMITH

FINDING DAYLIGHT

★ ★ ★

Nobody runs the football like Emmitt Smith. Other running backs may be faster. Others may be bigger. They may run more recklessly, trying to do it all by themselves. But Emmitt has the ability and the patience. He knows he can't do it alone. He knows how to wait for his blockers to open a hole in the other team's line. It's not easy to be patient while 300-pound bodies are crashing all around. But that's what makes Emmitt special. He waits for the moment when he can break free, then, whoosh . . . he's gone.

Emmitt led the National Football League in rushing three straight seasons. The first time was during only his second year in the league. In 1992-93, he became the first running back to lead the league in rushing and play for a Super Bowl champion in the same season. In 1993-94 he repeated this feat—*and* was named both the NFL's Most Valuable Player and Super Bowl MVP.

Emmitt is the best running back in football, but he knows how to fit into a team. His team, the Dallas Cowboys, is already being called the team of the '90s.

Still, Emmitt is always Emmitt. With all the pads and helmets, football can be a faceless game. But Emmitt is one of the easiest players to pick out on the field. He's smaller and faster than most players, but it's also the way he plays the game that sets him apart. Sportswriters have worked hard to describe his style, the way he moves his feet and dodges back and forth waiting for a hole to open up. One wrote that it looked as if Emmitt were playing hopscotch barefoot on a hot sidewalk. One of Emmitt's blockers, tackle Erik Williams, might have said it best: "Emmitt is our dancing bear. He's something special. We know that all he needs is just a little ounce of daylight."

Emmitt sidesteps some pursuing defenders.

Emmitt calls his running style "slow motion, waiting to see what develops." He says he is "constantly moving, low to the ground, trying to stay north and south." That means he doesn't like to race opposing players to the sidelines. He'd rather wait for his blockers to do their job, then go straight upfield. Emmitt knows how to get from here to there with no wasted effort—and with a lot of speed.

Emmitt J. Smith was born May 15, 1969, in Pensacola, Florida. His father, Emmitt Smith, Jr., was a city bus driver, and his mother, Mary, worked for a Pensacola bank. In addition to Emmitt, they raised three other sons—Erik, Emory, and Emil—and two daughters—Marsha and Connie. They made sure all their children had a solid upbringing and a firm set of values.

Emmitt showed early on that he was unique. He was crawling out of his crib at only nine months old. He was always playing with much older kids because he was physically advanced for his age. He could walk along curbs and even fences without falling off. He played tackle football with his cousins at the age of five, and at seven he moved on to organized football in the mini-mite division of the local children's league.

By the time Emmitt reached high school, he had grown almost to his full height of 5 feet 9 inches. He weighed only 175 pounds, but he was comfortable with what he could do on the football field. He was confident without being cocky. His coach at Escambia High School, Dwight Thomas, remembers meeting Emmitt for the first time: "All the other kids were acting like kids, fooling around, taking nothing seriously. Then a boy in neat, pressed clothes walks up to me and shakes my hand. 'Hi, Coach Thomas,' he said. So confident, so gracious." That was Emmitt.

Emmitt made the varsity team as a freshman and immediately established himself as the best runner around. And he got better every year. In many of his high-school games, Emmitt got his 100 yards without even carrying the ball 10 times.

Emmitt led Escambia to a 42-7 record during his high-school career. His team also won two Florida state championships. In his four high-school seasons, Emmitt ran for 8,804 yards. Only one player (Texas teenager Ken Hall in the early 1950s) ever collected more yardage in high school. Emmitt ran for at least 100 yards in 45 of his 49 games at Escambia, and in every game his junior and senior seasons. In one game during his junior year, he carried for 301 yards In some games, Escambia's opponents showed up with Emmitt's high-school number, 24, taped to their helmets. That didn't intimidate Emmitt—he dominated those games, too.

The amazing thing is, Emmitt could have run for even more yardage than he did. Coach Thomas taught his players good sportsmanship, and he also believed in playing everyone on the team. If Escambia built a huge lead, the starters would come out and the substitutes would get to play. That meant Emmitt went to the bench, but he never moped about it. "I'd take him out because we were so far ahead," Coach Thomas said, "and he'd be the biggest cheerleader on the bench."

"Records are made and then broken," said Emmitt. "They don't tell you what kind of football player you are. The way I see it, my talent came from God. What I add is my desire. I have great desire."

When he's not chewing up yardage on the field, Emmitt plays close attention to the game from the bench.

Emmitt resists being brought down by a defender.

Emmitt received a strong religious background from his mother. He got his athletic skill from his father. As a freshman and sophomore, Emmitt would usually play on Friday night, then return to the same field Saturday night to watch his dad play for Pensacola's semipro football team. Still, his dad never pressured him to play football. "His father didn't even want him to play at first," said Mary, Emmitt's mother. But once Emmitt started, his parents attended every game they could–right on into college and the pros.

In 1986, Emmitt visited the White House. He represented the nation's high-school football players in the "Just Say No to Drugs" campaign. Emmitt never tried drugs, and he also avoided gangs. "It just never occurred to me," he said.

Emmitt burst on to the college football scene by rushing for 224 yards in his first start as a Florida Gator.

Emmitt's performance in high school attracted a lot of interest from college recruiters. By the time he was ready to move on to college, he had filled out to 200 pounds, and he was able to lift 800 pounds with his legs. Still, some scouts doubted his ability. They said Emmitt wasn't fast enough or big enough to be a great college running back. One scouting service didn't even name him among the top 50 prospects in the nation.

"I know I'm not the fastest guy around," said Emmitt, "And I know I'm not the strongest guy either. It doesn't bother me at all. I see myself as being able to get the job done."

Emmitt chose to attend the University of Florida in nearby Gainesville. It didn't take him long to start getting the job done. Emmitt was named to start the third game of the season—a nationally televised game against Alabama. All he did was set a Florida record with 224 yards on 39 carries.

And it wasn't just what Emmitt did; it was how he did it. He never went in for talking trash or trying to show the other team up. He had been taught good sportsmanship, and that was how he played. One time, after scoring a touchdown, Emmitt did a celebration dance in the end zone. His dad spoke to him after the game. "We'll have no more of that," he said. Emmitt never did it again.

"He's a very mature, caring person," said his college coach, Galen Hall. "He cares most about his teammates."

And Emmitt rarely let them down. He topped 100 yards in 25 of his 34 games at Florida, and he got better every season. In his junior year, he ran for 316 yards in a single game. On that day, he broke Neal Anderson's career rushing record at Florida. Emmitt went on to amass 3,929 yards rushing–in just three years.

Dallas head coach Jimmy Johnson knew Emmitt was
a talent he could not pass up.

After Emmitt's record-breaking season, the NFL announced it would allow juniors to enter the draft of college players. Emmitt decided he would turn pro.

The year before, the Dallas Cowboys had been the worst team in the league, with a record of 1-15. They were rebuilding; they had traded their older players for draft choices. Dallas coach Jimmy Johnson had his eye on Emmitt. Johnson had tried to recruit Emmitt when he had coached the University of Miami football team, but Emmitt had picked Florida because they liked to run the ball, while Johnson liked to pass.

Now Johnson was in the pros. He knew he needed a well-rounded attack. He already had a good young quarterback in Troy Aikman. He wanted Emmitt to provide the running game. Dallas backfield coach Joe Brodsky ignored the scouts who said Emmitt wasn't big enough or fast enough. Brodsky knew there was a big difference between running on a track and running in a football game. He took one look at Emmitt and said, "He'll take your breath away, and you won't get it back until he scores."

The Cowboys had the top pick in the draft and used it to get another quarterback, Steve Walsh. They also had the 21st pick, which they'd gotten in a trade with the Minnesota Vikings. Dallas was hoping to use it on Emmitt.

Emmitt and teammate Troy Aikman

Emmitt talks with the press.

--- ★ ★ ★ ---

The Cowboys waited impatiently as teams made their first-round picks. After the 16th pick, Emmitt was still available. Dallas couldn't wait any longer. They worked a last-minute deal to get the Pittsburgh Steelers' 17th pick. The Cowboys then chose Emmitt.

Emmitt didn't leave college just to play pro football. He was determined to get a fair contract. Dallas's early offers didn't please Emmitt, so he refused to sign. He said he was going back to school to earn his degree in therapeutic recreation. He never let the negotiations get bitter or personal. He simply said he wanted a fair deal. (He would hold out again after Dallas's 1993 Super Bowl season. Again, he said he simply wanted what he was worth, compared to what other running backs were getting.)

Finally, after missing his rookie training camp and the exhibition season, Emmitt signed before the first game. The Cowboys needed him so badly that he was named the starting running back a week later.

The Cowboys had a lot of talented young players in 1990. But they were still trying to figure out how to win. Emmitt was the starting running back, but the Cowboys didn't know exactly how to use him. Emmitt had never complained or been outspoken. But now he made it clear. "I want the ball," he said. "I felt we had to run to take the pressure off Troy Aikman."

Emmitt ran for 100 yards in two of the next four games, and the Cowboys won all four of them. Dallas was suddenly 7-7 and fighting for a playoff spot. The Cowboys lost their last two games, missing the playoffs, but they had turned the corner. So had Emmitt.

Emmitt just missed 1,000 yards that year; he finished the season with 937 yards rushing. He scored 11 touchdowns and was named the Offensive Rookie of the Year. He also made the all-rookie team, and the Pro Bowl—football's All-Star game.

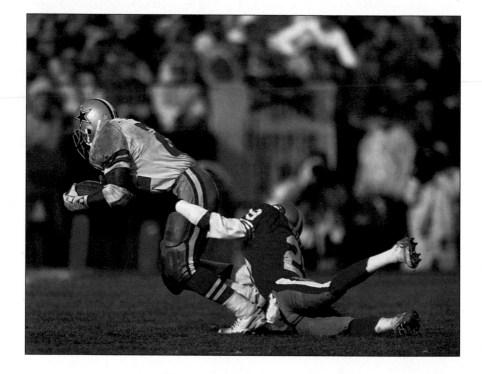

And he only got better. In only his second
season, Emmitt became the best running back
in the business. He led the league in rushing
with 1,563 yards. He scored 13 touchdowns.
But he also worked hard to fit into the balanced
Dallas offense. In his second year, he caught
49 passes. There was no stopping him.

There was no stopping the Cowboys, either. Quarterback Troy Aikman hurt his knee and missed the last four games, but with Emmitt helping to take up the slack, the Cowboys made the playoffs as a wild-card team, with a record of 11-5. They won their last five games. They advanced to meet the Chicago Bears in the playoffs, and Emmitt became first runner ever to burn the Bears for 100 yards in a playoff game. The Cowboys won, 17-13. That was it for Dallas, though. The Detroit Lions' defense shut down Emmitt and the Dallas offense in the next game, and the Cowboys lost.

Despite their playoff loss, it had been a great season. Emmitt had not only led the league in rushing, he was named starting running back for the National Football Conference in the Pro Bowl. He celebrated by giving all his offensive lineman Rolex watches. "No unit on this team has worked harder than the offensive line," Emmitt said. "They just keep working and eventually open lanes for me."

The next year, 1992, the Cowboys were determined to show everyone they were the best team in the league. Emmitt continued to improve. He became the first player since Eric Dickerson, eight years before, to lead the league in rushing in back-to-back seasons. He finished with 1,713 yards–the tenth-highest mark in NFL history. That also made him the first since Walter Payton to earn over 1,500 yards in back-to-back years. He was again named to start in the Pro Bowl. But Emmitt also improved in receiving. He led all NFC running backs in catches, with 59. He was the spearhead of the Dallas attack.

The Cowboys went 13-3 and won the NFC Eastern Division. In their first playoff game, they crushed the Philadelphia Eagles 34-10. Emmitt ran for 114 yards and a touchdown.

They advanced to meet the San Francisco 49ers in the NFC title game. The winner would go to the Super Bowl. The first half was close,

Emmitt gained 114 yards against the San Francisco 49ers in the 1992 NFC championship game.

tied 10-10. Then Dallas's youth and desire took over. The offensive line opened big holes for Emmitt and gave Aikman plenty of time to pass. "In the second half my boys just wore the 49ers down," said Emmitt. He finished with 114 yards rushing, seven catches and two touchdowns, as the Cowboys won 30-20.

Emmitt and Aikman thanked the linemen by buying airline tickets for them and their families to take vacations after the season. But that was still one game away. The Cowboys played the Buffalo Bills in Super Bowl XXVII. The Bills had lost the previous two Super Bowls and were hungry for victory. The Cowboys, however, were younger, stronger—and hungrier. They slaughtered the Bills 52-17. Emmitt ran for 108 yards and a touchdown.

The Cowboys kept up with tradition and poured Gatorade on coach Jimmy Johnson at the end of the game. But it was Emmitt

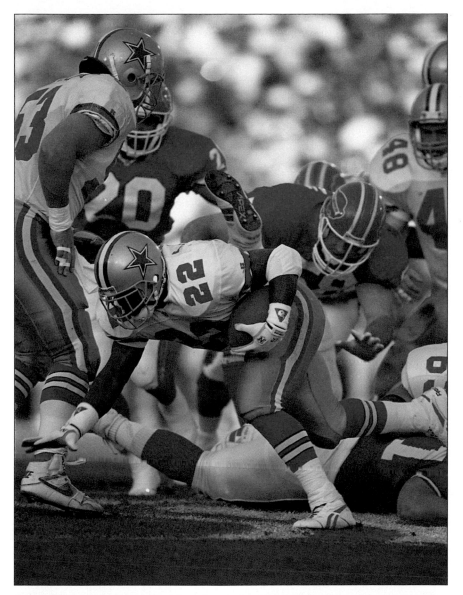

Emmitt helped lead the Cowboys to victory in Super Bowl XXVII.

who went up afterward and mussed coach Johnson's perfect hair. Everyone was smiling.

Cowboys fans smiled again in 1993-94, when Emmitt helped lead his team to another winning season—and then to another Super Bowl victory against the Buffalo Bills. During the season, he had earned his third straight rushing title, was named the NFL's Most Valuable Player, and was again voted to start in the Pro Bowl. During Super Bowl XXVIII, Emmitt ran for 132 yards and scored two touchdowns—and no one was surprised when he was named Super Bowl MVP.

Where will Emmitt end up? At the age of 24, he already had 5,699 career rushing yards. Walter Payton finished with 16,726 yards in 13 seasons—4,000 yards more than any other runner. It's too early to say Emmitt has a shot at Payton's record, but his running style is very similar to Payton's. And like Payton, he has piercing eyes that almost jump out of his helmet.

Many players and football experts agree that Emmitt's extraordinary vision is what makes him truly great. Emmitt agrees. "When I line up I don't see the wide receivers or the cornerbacks," he says. "But I see everybody on both teams. It's not a blur. It's a clear picture. I probably see things other people don't see. I can see changes in coverage. I can usually look at the defense and predict where the hole will be, regardless of where the play is called."

"Everybody talks about his great vision on the field," said his high-school coach, Dwight Thomas. "But where his success really comes from is how he sees himself. He's not searching for his identity, like so many kids. He's at ease."

Chronology

1969 – Emmitt J. Smith III is born in Pensacola, Florida, to Mary and Emmitt Smith, Jr.

1983 – Emmitt enters Escambia High School and, as a freshman, makes the varsity football team as starting tailback.

1986 – Emmitt finishes his high-school career with 8,804 yards rushing (No. 2 on the all-time list behind Ken Hall), an average of 7.8 yards a carry, and 106 touchdowns, while leading Escambia to two Florida state championships. He is named Prep Player of the Year by *Parade* magazine and *USA Today*.

1987 – Emmitt enters the University of Florida and starts the third game of the season. He reaches 1,000 yards in his seventh game—more quickly than any other runner in college history—and is named Freshman of the Year by United Press International and *The Sporting News*.

1989 – Emmitt sets a Florida record with a 316-yard game against New Mexico. His 1,599 yards on the season and 3,929 in his career also set school records. He is named an All-American and holds 58 Florida records.

--- ★ ★ ★ ---

1990 – Emmitt turns pro and is drafted in the first round with the 17th pick by the Dallas Cowboys. After a long holdout, Emmitt starts the second game of the season and goes on to run for 937 yards. He plays in the Pro Bowl.

1991 – Emmitt leads the NFL in rushing with 1,563 yards on 4.3 yards a carry. At 22 years and 7 months, he is the youngest player in NFL history to reach 1,500 yards. He is named starting running back in the Pro Bowl.

1992 – Emmitt leads the NFL with 1,713 yards rushing, becoming the first since Eric Dickerson to claim back-to-back rushing titles and the first since Walter Payton to rush or 1,500 yards in back-to-back seasons.

1993 – The Cowboys win Super Bowl XXVII 52-17 over the Buffalo Bills, making Emmitt the first running back to lead the NFL in rushing and win a championship in the same season. He starts his second straight Pro Bowl.

1994 – Emmitt earns his third straight rushing title, is named The NFL's Most Valuable Player, and starts his third straight Pro Bowl. He helps lead the Cowboys to a 30-13 victory over the Buffalo Bills in Super Bowl XXVIII and is named Super Bowl MVP.

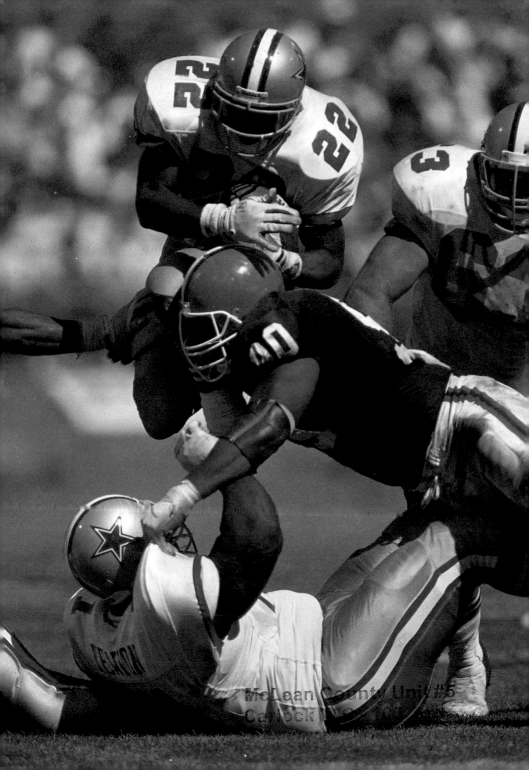

★ ★ ★

About the Author

Ted Cox is a Chicago journalist who works at the *Daily Southtown*. He has covered sports for the Chicago *Reader* and *Chicago* magazine. He worked at United Press International and holds a B.S. in journalism from the University of Illinois at Urbana-Champaign. He lives in Chicago with his wife, Catherine, and their daughter, Sadie.